John Patrick Norman McHennessy, the boy who was always late

I must not Tell lies about crocodiles and I must not lose my gloves
I must not tell lies about crocodiles and I must not lose my glov
I must not tell lies about crocodiles and I must not lose my glo
I must not tell lies about crocodiles and I must not lose my gloves
I must not tell lies about crocodiles and I must not lose my gloves
I must not tell lies about crocodiles and I most not lose my glove
I must not tell lies about crocodiles and I must not lose my glov
I must not tell lies about crocodiles and I must not lose my glove
I must not tell lies about crocodiles and I must not lose my glov
I must not tell lies about crocodiles and I must not lose my gloves
I must not tell lies about crocodiles and I must not lose my gloves
I must not tell lies about crocodiles and I must not lose my gloves
I must not tell lies about crocodiles and I must not lose my gloves
I must not tell lies about crocodiles and I must not lose my gloves
I must not tell lies about crocodiles and I must not love my gloves
I must not tell lies about crocodiles and I must not lose my gloves
I must not tell lies about crocodiles and I must not lose my gloves
I must not tell lies about crocodiles and I must not lose my gloves
I must not tell lies about crocodiles and I must not lose my gloves
I must not tell lies about crocodiles and I must not lose my gloves
I must not tell lies about crocodiles and I must not lose my glove
I must not tell lies about crocodiles and I must not lose my gloves
I must not tell lies about crocodiles and I must not lose my gloves
I must not tell lies about crocodiles and I must not lose my glove
I must not tell lies about crocodiles and I must not lose my gloves
I must not tell lies about crocodiles and I must not lose my gloves

I must not tell lise about crocodiles and I must nat lose my gloves
I must not tell lise about crocodiles and I must not lose my gloves
I must not tell lise about crocodiles and I must not lose my gloves
I mustnot tell lise about crocodiles and I mustnot lose my gloves
I must not tell lise about crocodiles and I must not lose my gloves
I must not tell lise about crocodiles and I must not lose my gloves
I must not tell lise about crocodiles and I must not lose my gloves
I must not tell lise about crocodiles and I must not lose my gloves
I must not tell lise about crocodiles and I must not lose my gloves
must not tell lise about crocodiles and I must not lose my gloves
must not tell lise about crocodiles and I must not lose my gloves
must not tell lise about crocodiles and I must not lose my gloves
must not tell lise about crocodiles and I must not lose my gloves
must not tell lise about crocodiles and I must not lose my gloves
must not tell lise about crocodiles and I must not lose my gloves
I mustnot tell lise about crocodiles and I must not lose my gloves
I must not tell lise about crocodiles and I must not lose my gloves
I must not tell lise about crocodiles and I most not lose my gloves
I must not tell lise about crocodiles and I must not lose my gloves
I must not tell lise about crocodiles and I must not lose my gloves
must not tell lise about croodiles and I must not dose my gloves
most not tell lise about crocodilesand I must not lose my gloves
I mustnot tell lise about crocodiles and I mustnot lose my gloves
I must not tell lise about crocodiles and I must not lose my gloves
I must not tell lise about crocodiles and must not lose mygloves
I must not tell lise about crocodiles and must not lose my gloves

Other books by John Burningham

John Burningham

John Patrick Norman McHennessy, the boy who was always late

RED FOX

ut sementem feceris, ita metes

A Red Fox Book

Published by Random House Children's Books
61-63 Uxbridge Road, London W5 5SA

A division of The Random House Group Ltd
Addresses for companies within The Random House
Group Limited can be found
at: www.randomhouse.co.uk/offices.htm

7 9 10 8

First published in Great Britain by
Jonathan Cape Ltd 1987
Red Fox edition 2000

THE RANDOM HOUSE GROUP Ltd Reg. No. 954009
www.kidsatrandomhouse.co.uk

978 0 099 75200 4

Printed in Singapore

John Patrick Norman McHennessy set off along the
road to learn.

On the way a crocodile came out of a drain and got hold of his satchel.

John Patrick Norman McHennessy pulled and pulled but the crocodile would not let go.

He threw a glove into the air and the crocodile snapped at the glove and let go of the satchel.

John Patrick Norman McHennessy hurried along the road to learn but the crocodile had made him late.

"John Patrick Norman McHennessy, you are late and where is your other glove?"

"I am late, Sir, because on the way a crocodile came out of a drain and got hold of my satchel, and would only let go when I threw my glove, which he ate."

"There are no crocodiles living in the drains around here. You are to stay in late and write out 300 times, 'I must not tell lies about crocodiles and I must not lose my glove.'"

So John Patrick Norman McHennessy stayed in late and wrote out 300 times, "I must not tell lies about crocodiles and I must not lose my glove."

John Patrick Norman McHennessy hurried off along the road to learn.

But on the way a lion came out of the bushes and tore his trousers.

He managed to climb up a tree. He stayed up the tree until the lion lost interest in him and went away.

John Patrick Norman McHennessy hurried off along the road to learn but he was late because of the lion.

"You are late again, John Patrick Norman McHennessy, and you have torn your trousers."

"I am late, Sir, because on my way here a lion jumped out of the bushes and tore my trousers and I had to climb a tree and wait until the lion went away."

"There are no such things as lions in the bushes around here. You are to stand in the corner and say out loud 400 times, 'I must not tell lies about lions and I must not tear my trousers.'"

John Patrick Norman McHennessy stood in the corner and said out loud 400 times, "I must not tell lies about lions and I must not tear my trousers."

John Patrick Norman McHennessy hurried off along the
road to learn.

But on the way, as he was crossing the bridge over the river, a huge tidal wave swept him off his feet.

He managed to cling on to the rail until the wave had passed and the water had gone down.

John Patrick Norman McHennessy hurried along the road to learn but he was late because of the tidal wave.

"You are late again, John Patrick Norman McHennessy, and your clothes are wet."

"I am late, Sir, because on my way here, as I was crossing the bridge, a tidal wave swept me off my feet and made me wet and I had to cling on to the rail until the water went down."

"There are no such things as tidal waves in the rivers around here that sweep people off the bridges. You will be locked in until you have written down 500 times, 'I must not tell lies about tidal waves in the river and I must not get my clothes wet.' And if you keep telling these lies and being late I may have to hit you with my stick."

So John Patrick Norman McHennessy was locked in until he had written down 500 times, "I must not tell lies about tidal waves in the river and I must not get my clothes wet."

John Patrick Norman McHennessy hurried along the
road to learn.

On the way nothing happened and he was able to be on time.

"John Patrick Norman McHennessy, I am being held up in the roof by a great big hairy gorilla. You are to get me down at once."

"There are no such things as great big hairy gorillas in
the roofs around here, Sir."

And so John Patrick Norman McHennessy set off along
the road to learn.

I must not Tell lies about crocodiles and I must not lose my gloves
I must not tell lies about crocodiles and I must not lose my glove
I must not tell lies about crocodiles and I must not lose my glo
I must not tell lies about crocodiles and I must not lose my gloves
I must not tell lies about crocodiles and I must not lose my gloves
I must not tell lies about crocodiles and I must not lose my glove
I must not tell lies about crocodiles and I must not lose my glov
I must not tell lies about crocodiles and I must not lose my glov
I must not tell lies about crocodiles and I must not lose my glov
I must not tell lies about crocodiles and I must not lose my gloves
I must not tell lies about crocodiles and I must not lose my gloves
I must not tell lies about crocodiles and I must not lose my gloves
I must not tell lies about crocodiles and I must not lose my gloves
I must not tell lies about crocodiles and I must not lose my gloves
I must not tell lies about crocodiles and I must not lose my gloves
I must not tell lies about crocodiles and I must not love my gloves
I must not tell lies about crocodiles and I must not lose my gloves
I must not tell lies about crocodiles and I must not lose my gloves
I must not tell lies about crocodiles and I must not lose my gloves
I must not tell lies about crocodiles and I must not lose my gloves
I must not tell lies about crocodiles and I must not lose my gloves
I must not tell lies about crocodiles and I must not lose my gloves
I must not tell lies about crocodiles and I must not lose my gloves
I must not tell lies about crocodiles and I must not lose my glove
I must not tell lies about crocodiles and I must not lose my gloves
I must not tell lies about crocodiles and I must not lose my gloves

I must not tell lise about crocodiles and I must not lose my gloves
I must not tell lise about crocodiles and I must not lose my gloves
I must not tell lise about crocodiles and I must not lose my gloves
I must not tell lise about crocodiles and I must not lose my gloves
I must not tell lise about crocodiles and I must not lose my gloves
I must not tell lise about crocodiles and I must not lose my gloves
must not tell lise about crocodiles and I must not lose my gloves
must not tell lise about crocodiles and I must not lose my gloves
must not tell lise about crocodiles and I must not lose my gloves
must not tell lise about crocodiles and I must not lose my gloves
must not tell lise about crocodiles and I must not lose my gloves
must not tell lise about crocodiles and I must not lose my gloves
must not tell lise about crocodiles and I must not lose my gloves
must not tell lise about crocodiles and I must not lose my gloves
must not tell lise about crocodiles and I must not lose my gloves
I must not tell lise about crocodiles and I must not lose my gloves
I must not tell lise about crocodiles and I must not lose my gloves
I must not tell lise about crocodiles and I must not lose my gloves
I must not tell lise about crocodiles and I must not lose my gloves
I must not tell lise about crocodiles and I must not lose my gloves
I must not tell lise about croodiles and I must not lose my gloves
most not tell lise about crocodilesand I must not lose my gloves
I must not tell lise about crocodiles and I must not lose my gloves
I must not tell lise about crocodiles and must not lose my gloves
I must not tell lise about crocodiles and must not lose my gloves
I must not tell lise about crocodiles and must not lose my gloves